B-SCAMMER!!! Do You Care For Square Shooter???

#3 Prevailing Forms of Innovative Bitcoin Scams

PUSHPARAJ KULOOR SHETTY

B-Scam

The definition of **Scam** as per the Dictionary.com is a confidence game or other fraudulent scheme, especially for making a quick profit; swindle.

Now let me explain, the **B-Scam** as you guessed it rightly; refers to **Bitcoin Scam**!!

As I am writing this book, some of you already trapped by those Innovative Scammers or You yet to make a move under confusion state and It's not your fault!

It's just a curiosity to make easy money to pay-off your burden and lead a debt-free life.

Ultimately everyone needs the same, that's a universal truth and the same intentions being trapped by the Scammers with the help of latest technology & social media platforms.

Source of B-Scams

The easiest way to Scam people is through **FACEBOOK** (**FB**), because of it's vast Social Reachability. Thanks, Mr Mark Zuckerberg for his utmost effort to curtail down the overall Negative Campaign in **FB**. His good intention to connect people using the Internet, being taken advantage by Scammers.

The Scammer always keeps an eye on people's data, so he or she searches a **FB** group which involves most engagements.

The Scammer starts with a simple & attractive post in a **FB** group and engages the group members to "**ASK HOW**" campaign in the comment section or Private Messenger. These campaigns short-lived, until someone reports to **FB**.

Now it's Scammers turn to engage you through **WHATSAPP** or **TELEGRAM** apps which are convenient to continue the conversations, thanks to its end to end encryptions.

How To Confirm A Scammer?

- ❖ The Scammer always does exceptional things to hide their true identity.

- ❖ The Scammer set their privacy with the utmost importance in **FB**.

- ❖ The Scammer display fake human faces like Blonde pics, African Ladies pic or Bitcoin Mining machine pics to get attention.

- ❖ The Scammer starts their conversation with pleasingly to convince and gives you a positive vibe as much as possible.

- ❖ The Scammer diverts your attention if he or she gets blocked in **FB**, saying their account gets hacked.

- ❖ The Scammer ensures you to join their WhatsApp Business Account (**Which not verified by the WhatsApp**), to convince you that they are 100% legit.

- ❖ The Scammer creates a **TELEGRAM GROUP** in which all participants get blocked to communicate each other & only an admin(**SCAMMER**) can post messages or pictures or videos to attract group members with fake testimonials or Blockchain transactions or Payout **GIF** screenshots with recent date & time.

- ❖ The Scammer can also divert you to their Company Websites to ensure you, continue to invest (**fake investment**) with them using Bitcoin Wallets.

- ❖ The Scammer ensures you to get a Bitcoin Wallet using genuine Bitcoin Apps like Paxful, Coinbase, Blockchain Wallets, etc. to make you feel safe and authentic.

- ❖ The Scammer relies on majorly Bitcoin transactions, which is safer to hide their identity since there is No

Central Authority to verify the same. Others use **SKRILL**, which is also a payment app, more comfortable to set up using your email I'd (**NO PROOF REQUIRED**).

❖ The Scammer grabs attention by creating a fake customer service using WhatsApp Business Account, personating Investment Company which never exist.

Bitcoin & Its Real Purpose

Bitcoin(**BTC**) uses Peer-to-Peer(**P2P**) technology to operate with No Central Authority or banks; managing transactions and the issuing of Bitcoins is carried out collectively by the network.

Bitcoin is open-source; its design is public, nobody owns or controls Bitcoin, and everyone can take part.

Bitcoin is a cryptocurrency (**Digital Asset**). It is a decentralised digital currency without a central bank or single administrator that can be sent from user to user on **P2P** Bitcoin network without the need for intermediaries.

Bitcoin formerly knows to be developed by an unknown person or group of people using the name Satoshi Nakamoto in the Year 2008, and initial release is done on 9 January 2009, in a domain name (**Website**) called www.bitcoin.org

Bitcoins created as a reward for a process known as Mining. The miners can choose which transactions to process and prioritise those that pay higher fees.

The Bitcoin transactions are verified by network nodes through cryptography and recorded in public distributed ledger called a Blockchain. It implemented as a chain of blocks, each block containing a Hash (**SHA-256 Cryptographic Hash**) of the previous block up to the genesis block (**first block of a Blockchain**) of the chain. A network of communicating nodes running Bitcoin software maintains the Blockchain.

Satoshi (**named after Bitcoin's creator**) is the smallest amount within Bitcoin, representing 0.00000001 Bitcoins, One Hundred Millionth of a Bitcoin.

In the Blockchain, Bitcoins registered to Bitcoin addresses. Creating a Bitcoin address requires picking a random valid Private Key and computing the corresponding Bitcoin address.

9

This computation can be done in a split second (**a very brief moment**). But the reverse, computing the Private Key of a given Bitcoin address, is practically unfeasible, simply means it's impossible.

The purpose of the Bitcoin system is simply to allow people to store and transfer money (**BTC**) securely. So, Bitcoin is the Banking and Payment system. Bitcoin can be used to buy or sell items from people and companies that accept Bitcoin as payment.

SOURCE: www.wikipedia.com

How Scammer do their Business?

Now let's look at some innovative Scammers website, which makes you believe that it's genuine.

Welcome to Infinite-Mining

BEST TO START BITCOIN MINING TODAY! Join over 3.000.000 people with the world's leading hashpower provider Daily and Instant Withdrawals.

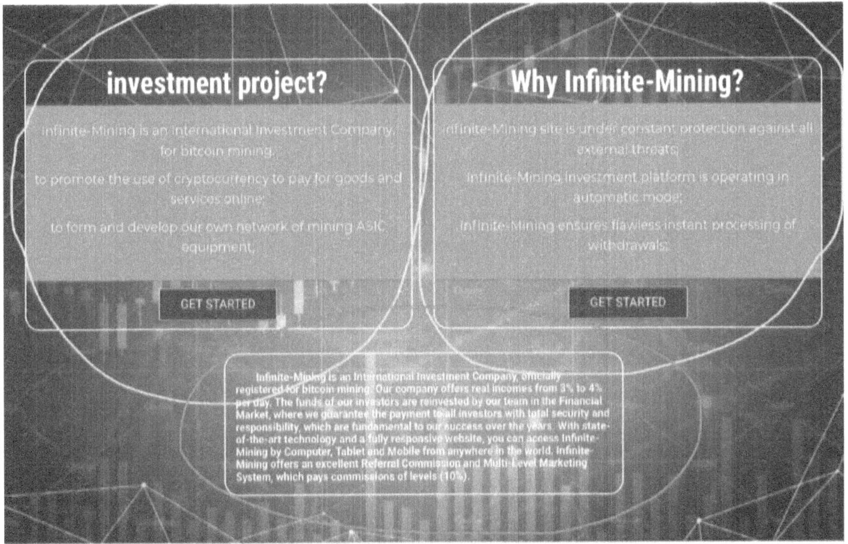

Who We Are

...it. Message us ...officially registered and conducts ...ancing activities under existing United Kingdom legislation. The necessary information about the company

Why Trade With Us

Who We Are

Infinite-Mining was officially registered and conducts financing activities under existing United Kingdom legislation. The necessary information about the company can be found on our website or in the official sources.

Our Aim

Having seen the conditions of the people financially,we are aimed at improving lives in the best way we can by been very vast and current on market trends..Many people have been seeking for a better life hence the reason why we put up this innovation to to impact positively

Join Us Today

1. Register your Account
2. Choose the most suitable plan for yourself
3. Make a deposit and watch your funds grow
4. Make a withdrawal every 5days and get it credited within 48hours
5. Invite friends and family to earn bonus

JOIN NOW   **FOLLOW US ON TELEGRAM**

Why Trade With Us

$ NO DEPOSIT CHARGE
Unlike most brokers,we do not charge a dime on any deposit made by our clients

DEPOSIT CONFIRMATION
It takes less than 24hours for a deposit to be confirmed

CAPITAL GUARANTEE
On any case of bad trade,capital would be made available to clients

$ CONTRACT TERMINATION
Each client has the right to cancel a contract of which the accrued profits will be minused and a 5% charge upon withdrawal.

$ SEMINARS
We host seminars chaired by the CEO every fixed moment in any choice location within the country

Frequently Asked Questions

❓ How can I register an account?

❓ Is there age restriction for this program?

❓ When can I make a deposit?

❓ When can I make a withdrawal?

❓ Can I terminate a running contract?

❓ How safe is my investment?

Ans: You can register an account here www.infinite-mining.xyz (Click to massage us)

(Send Massage)

Message us

#1. B-Scam using a Website

Do you observe anything unusual in the above screenshot of a particular Scammer?

Yes, **XYZ** is a new domain that can give your website a bold new look.

The **XYZ** domain extensions are very inexpensive to buy and maintain. Hence Scammers, Phishers and Hacker jumped to use these domains to Scam people.

Mostly when you visit these site, a pop-up message will display their **Bitcoin Wallet address** to transfer the fund(**BTC**) to invest and also cautions you not to move the fund to any other wallet address, so that you feel that its a genuine company.

In the above website, as you noticed, the Scammer created such an elegant page setup, which you will fall prey without further thinking. The wording on the website is neat and grammatically sturdy!!!

The Scammer also creates a fake testimonial to look & feel more trustworthy investment company on the earth. You will end up in investing with them, no other questions asked!!!

Once Scammer approaches you to ensure that you have a Bitcoin Wallet address, if not, the Scammer starts guiding you create a wallet address using a legitimate Android or iPhone Bitcoin Wallet App to convince you to believe them blindly, since Bitcoin Wallet App required a valid Photo & Address verification, which builds confidence to continue business with them!!!

The Scammer informs you to register your details on their website as part of an initial setup, which you will agree to do so by seeing a clean and attractive website page.

After you finish your Bitcoin Wallet address, the Scammer informs you to deposit $100 (**worth BTC**) into their given wallet address. The Scammer tries to please you with an initial $50 offer as part of investment promotion, that means you only need to deposit $50 worth **BTC** instead of $100. So cool right! Now you agree with the Scammer since it's lower investment plan!

As the Scammer promised, your $100 investment converted to $1500 within 24 hrs!!!

The Scammer engages you with screenshot tactics, asking you to share the profit page screenshot, and tells you to keep an eye on your profit, specifying their company follows that method.

Now the game starts!

As per the instructions you always login their website & share the screenshot to the Scammer and One beautiful day, your login details get blocked by the website saying wrong credentials and force you to personal chat with the Scammer.

The Scammer informs you that you have to upgrade your investment plan with a nominal fee, you in-turn agree to do so, since it's the lower amount and going to get a huge profit!

Once you do transfer the fund, your account reinstated to the original state. The Scammer convinces you with positive note and updates you that your Mining started by the system, no need to worry since your profit is safe with us.

Now, fake Mining continues to run by their system and doesn't stop at $1500 profit; you will start a Private chat with the Scammer about the issue and try to convince you that leftover Bitcoins being taken out (**mined**) by the system.

Your profit may be increase to $10000 or $20000 depends on their need in a day or two!!! You are happier to see the result as promised by the Scammer.

Once so-called fake Mining stops at $10000 or $20000, the Scammer asks you to pay their commission of 20% on the profit as soon as possible to withdraw the fund. When you question the Scammer regarding the commission, he will convince you saying it's part of our company policy & it's normal. If you try to bargain, the Scammer specifies your huge profit gain.

If you stop here, you will save your hard-earned money. Otherwise, get ready to lose your hard earn money within no time.

The Scammer will use their full energy to convince you to pay the amount and get the fund released immediately.

Imagine if you agree to pay them so-called commission, the Scammer sends you the email to congratulate you and nominate you as their agent in your country to get more profit in their company.

Next step of the Scammer is to tell you to withdraw the fund(**profit**) from the website, for the process the Scammer keeps engage you with screenshots so that you won't get any doubt on them.

The Scammer sends you another email saying your profit withdrawn successfully. Now you need to pay transfer charges, say 10% of profit to get transfer the Bitcoin from the machine. You May ask the Scammer regarding this and get an argument with the Scammer. If he is not able to convince you, transfer your communication to their customer care (**handled by the same person**), which may give you more definite answers.

Now the Scammer understands clearly about you if you agree to pay them more to get the profit. Further force you to pay the Conversion charges, say 10% of profit which never specified before. The Scammer doesn't stop here. They start sending the videos & pics regarding the Bitcoin converting machine, along with Bitcoin technical words like Hash conversions to confuse you and stay with them. They may start sending you the images of **MINING MACHINE** and **CONVERTING MACHINE**, to engage you with them.

By this time, you end up spending a considerable amount with the Scammer in a short period,the Scammer ensures to keep the momentum. And finally update saying that your Bitcoin now transferred and converting to Hash keys, which will transfer to your Blockchain wallet.

As the Scammer promised, sends you a **QR CODE** to scan into your Blockchain Imported Address. That means, you will get the fund into your wallet as **NON-SPENDABLE FUND**, simply called **WATCH ONLY ADDRESS**.

These funds, as name specify, cannot be spent by you until you get a **PRIVATE KEY** for that address. In other words, **NON-SPENDABLE FUND** is not a safe amount in your wallet, since the Scammer having its Private Key and full authority to withdraw fund in it.

Now it's a crucial moment for you!!! You got the fund in your wallet without a Private Key. You forced to approach the Scammer to get the Private Key. Meanwhile, the person introduced you to this investment may disappear saying his mobile lost and company arrange new mobile(**ultimately from your money!**).

The customer care person approaches you again for Private Key fees worth $1000. If you deny to pay the Scammer gives an option pay only $500 to get the Private Key!

The Scammer ensures you to arrange the amount for Private Key to get the fund immediately. After Scammer may tell you that our company person already went to Head Office(**never exist**) to get the Private Key. Then the next two days Scammers will keep quiet. If you force then for the Private Key, the Scammer informs you that the person who went collect your Private Key is missing for two days and **FBI** behind him to trace. Ultimately you end up losing your entire hard earn money by your mere foolishness.

It's the end of the Scammers game. Simply, Your money becomes their profit!!!

#2. NON-SPENDABLE FUND (NSF) or WATCH ONLY Scam

The **NSF** or **WATCH ONLY WALLET ADDRESS** recovery experts are another form of Bitcoin Scammers.

After you lose your money for Bitcoin Investment Scammers, you may search google for how to recover **NSF**.

bitcoin private key hack

bitcoin private key hack : Are you looking for a reliable bitcoin private key hack service? Advanced bitcoin hack tools, Private key hack, Bitcoin generators, Bitcoin fake transaction Generators, Bitcoin silent miner, Block-chain account recovery tool, Non-spendable fund hack. SOFTWARE AVAILABLE

We will give you specifically the following, bitcoin private key finder online tools, this tools will help you to recover lost bitcoin funds from personal/random and dormant wallet addresses and we advice that you do not use our tools the wrong way. Bitcoin private key finder 2019 is the latest version of the available tools and what this tool does differently is that is faster more reliable and apply additional security to cover or hid your tracks form any 3rd party trackers.

WHAT IS A WATCH ONLY ADDRESS?

WHAT IS A WATCH ONLY ADDRESS?
A watch-only address is any bitcoin receive
address that has funds in the wallet but can

This tool is strictly for educational purposes. functions exactly as seen in the video you can reach me for more information and direct contact below.

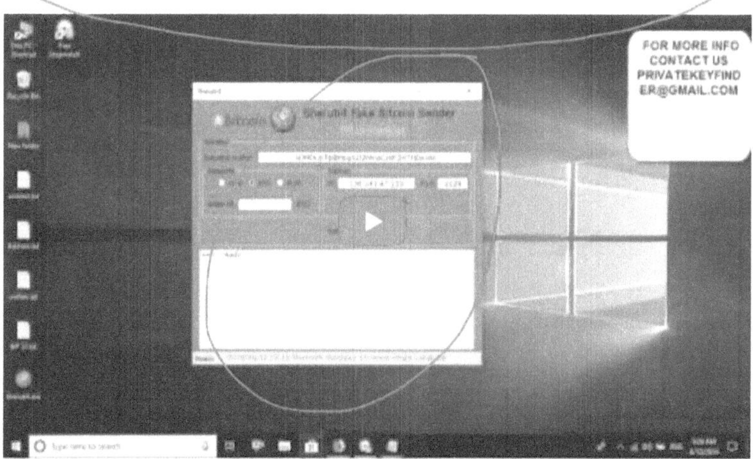

Private key hack

This is the best way to make easy and fast cash without having to stress yourself. anyone can do this anytiime.

Silent miner

Silent miners can get you some free coins but slowlv. install this software in

Send fake bitcoins

Prank a friend family or love once. send them a fake bitcoin transaction into their wallet and tell them you sent them money to see their reaction.

Clipboard virus

am sure most of you have fallen victim for this when vou send bitcoins ass you

For an example, the above website will lead you to their YouTube Channel to get a glimpse of the technique used to recover the **NSF**. The video will force you to get glued since it has no audio in it.

The Scammer maintains his patience until you approach him for his help. Once you start chatting with him through WhatsApp or a TELEGRAM, the Scammer ensures you to trust him. If you do so, the Scammer asks for his small nominal fee. Once you pay, the Scammer guides to watch his YouTube tutorial to get more convinced.

The Scammer may inform you that he is doing this to help you with no other intentions. If you got convinced, he would further force you to download his software intended for using Google Drive. If you install the software in your Windows **PC**, the Scammer now gets full access to your system and can copy your data also.

Next step of the Scammer may force you to follow steps as shown in his YouTube tutorial, and ask you to create a **PRIVATE KEY** for your **NSF** address. The software will generate a fake Private Key, which not related to your current **NSF** address, actually displays a wallet address linked to the Scammer and has got its full access.

The Scammer may also follow up with you on WhatsApp audio call to maintain his authenticity. He will further guide to import the newly created address into your a Blockchain wallet. When you import a new wallet address into your Blockchain app, the corresponding Private Key also displayed. Meanwhile, the Scammer made a copy of the same using your system via Private **Virtual Protocol Network** (**VPN**), provided by the Scammer.

Using a Standard Bitcoin Rate Calculator, the Scammer makes you calculate 10% of the value of current Bitcoin Price, corresponding to your **NSF** wallet value in **USD($)**, which is a significant amount to spend. The Scammer informs you that 10% of the cost of Satoshi required to activate the new wallet so that **NSF** wallet gets activated automatically.

The Scammer informs you to get arranged the fund and update him by taking sufficient time. If you say you don't have enough fund for the same, the Scammer will come forward for financial help to make you feel safer & trustworthy.

Meanwhile, the Scammer will transfer some funds into a newly created wallet and withdraws immediately, when you inactive in mobile to make you believe that funds start pouring in through newly formed portfolio.

When you enquire the Scammer regarding the received fund in the new wallet, he will divert your attention and convince you that your wallet partially active, hence the fund not getting deposited. Accordingly, the Scammer asks you to arrange the fund immediately to activate the wallet and enjoy your fund.

If you request the Scammer regarding the financial help, he will come forward with an offer 50% whatever the required amount. When you agree to arrange some fund, the Scammer ensures you to update him the transaction details with a screenshot.

The Scammer tactically make-believe him and assures you that your fund will be safe in that wallet and inform you transfer it immediately to other Bitcoin wallets, which will be a more reliable method.

As per the Scammer guarantee, if you ready for Satoshi transfer, the Scammer tells you to transfer right away, so that rest of the necessary fund will be transferred by him simultaneously.

If you transfer the said amount, the Scammer immediately withdraws using the Private Key with him and inform you that the wallet not yet activated and you further need to arrange funds to enable the same quickly.

The Scammer won't give you any further time for thinking and threaten you to send more funds in no time. The Scammer makes sure to believe him for helping hand to recover your fund. But it's not the fact.

The Scammer's intention to get the fund in the form of Bitcoins as soon as possible in the name of so-called **NSF RECOVERY** And it's the latest gimmick to fool you with the latest technology in a fraction of time to get them easy money.

#3. B-Scam in TELEGRAM

The Binary Trading Option is a prevalent Bitcoin Scam in TELEGRAM, thanks to it's an end to end encryption. The Scammer initially uses a **FB GROUP** platform to attract people who search for easy money option. When a person interacts with their **FB** post, asks him to join their TELEGRAM Channel.

The TELEGRAM Channel mostly having subscribers, which added by the scamming person itself or person joins through their add link. The channel's privacy enabled such as way that

NONE of the members in the group can communicate with each other, only admin (**Scammer**), can control everything.

The Scammer mostly hides his contact number, sets only a personal name to reach out quickly to its prey members!!!

Once you get into the TELEGRAM Channel, you start getting investment plan details, testimonials, payout intimation (**everything fake**) to encourage you to start investing immediately. To do that you force to Private chat with the Scammer, he will convince such a way that no stone unturned.

Once you agree to invest as per the Scammer fake investment plan, the Scammer ensures you have a Bitcoin Wallet or **SKRILL** account. These are the convenient and safer mode of payment for the Scammer. The credit card mode of payment can be reversed to a source of the original transaction if you fall prey to such Scammer within 120 days, so the majority of avoids it.

As the Scammer's promise, your investment now converted to ten times of original investment!!!

Now again it's the Scammer's turn to drop you a screenshot of your profit and congratulate you for the same. The Scammer uses a website called **IQ OPTION WIKI**, which is purely created by fans of **IQ OPTION (an investment platform)** and not created or related to **IQ OPTION** at all.

Using **IQ OPTION WIKI**, the Scammer creates your profile in it and do necessary changes accordingly to your data and takes a screenshot to share you. The screenshot looks lively to convince you & force you to pay their 15% commissions. If you agree to continue to pay, the Scammer may disappear for sometime after confirming your payment.

The Scammer returns after a while and mostly inform you that your profit now increases further and to release the fund, you need to bear further amount immediately, and the game continues for higher profits...!!!

How To Avoid Scammer?

> Never join a **FB** group, created by unknown people, even though compelling you to do so. Restrict your Social Media engagements for essential things like General Knowledge updating only.

> Always use **TWO-FACTOR AUTHENTICATION (2FA)** using a trusted app calle **AUTHY**, which can be download from the given link *www.authy.com.*

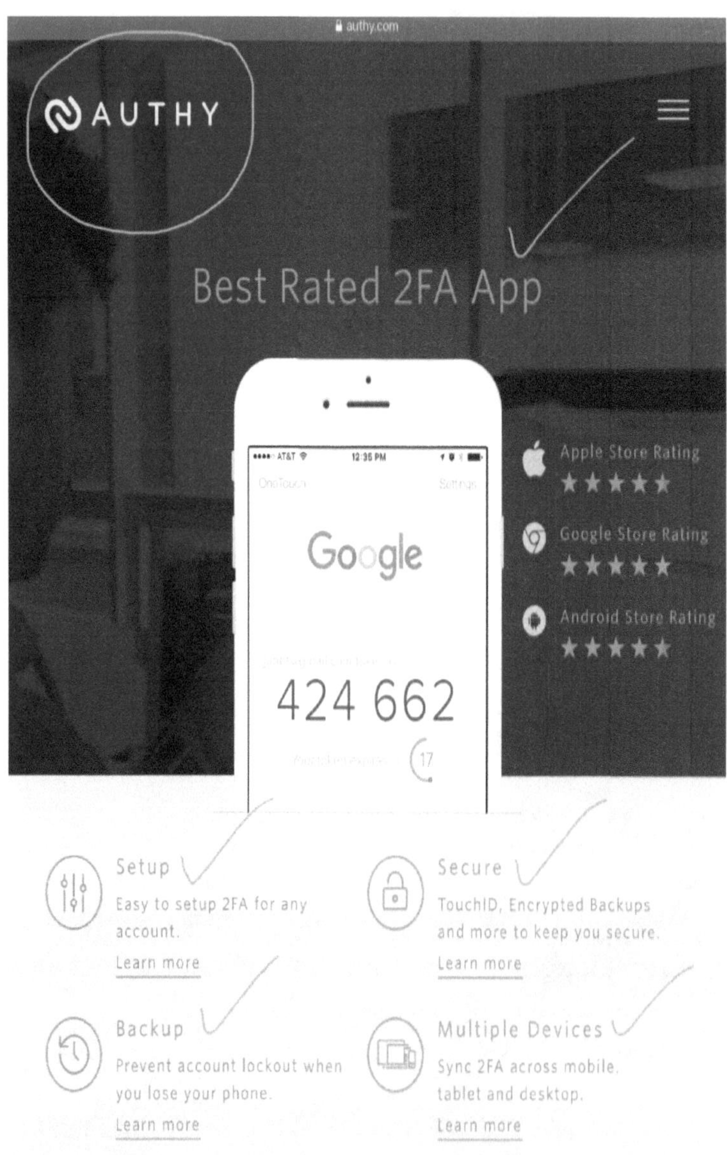

authy.com
AUTHY
Best Rated 2FA App
Google
424 662
Apple Store Rating
Google Store Rating
Android Store Rating
Setup
Easy to setup 2FA for any account.
Learn more
Secure
TouchID, Encrypted Backups and more to keep you secure.
Learn more
Backup
Prevent account lockout when you lose your phone.
Learn more
Multiple Devices
Sync 2FA across mobile, tablet and desktop.
Learn more

➢ Never forget to secure your **GMAIL** or other email platforms and all major **Bitcoin** wallet Apps with a **2FA** using AUTHY (**Highly recommended than Google Authenticator due to its backup option**) immediately, to avoid significant Scammers.

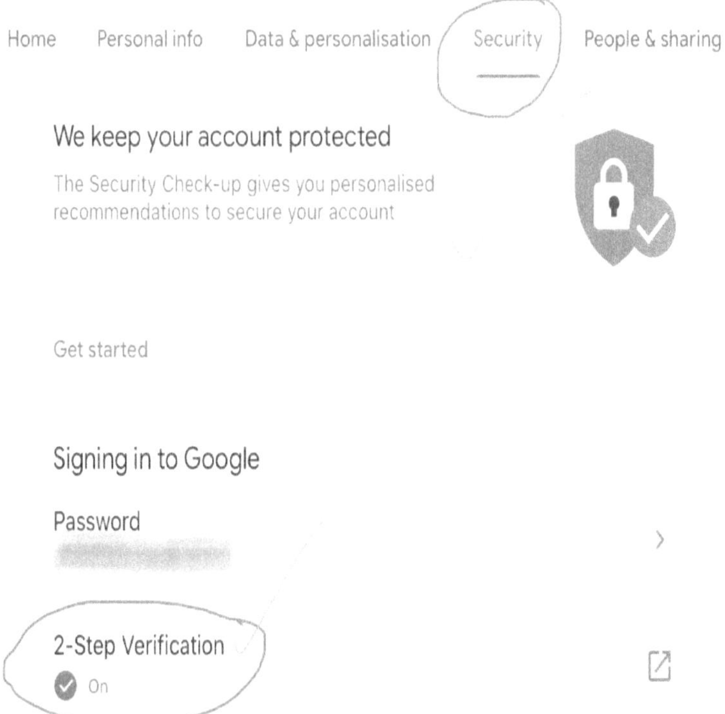

➢ To secure your email or wallet accounts, simply go to the Security Section inside the settings and scan the **QR CODE** to Authenticate.

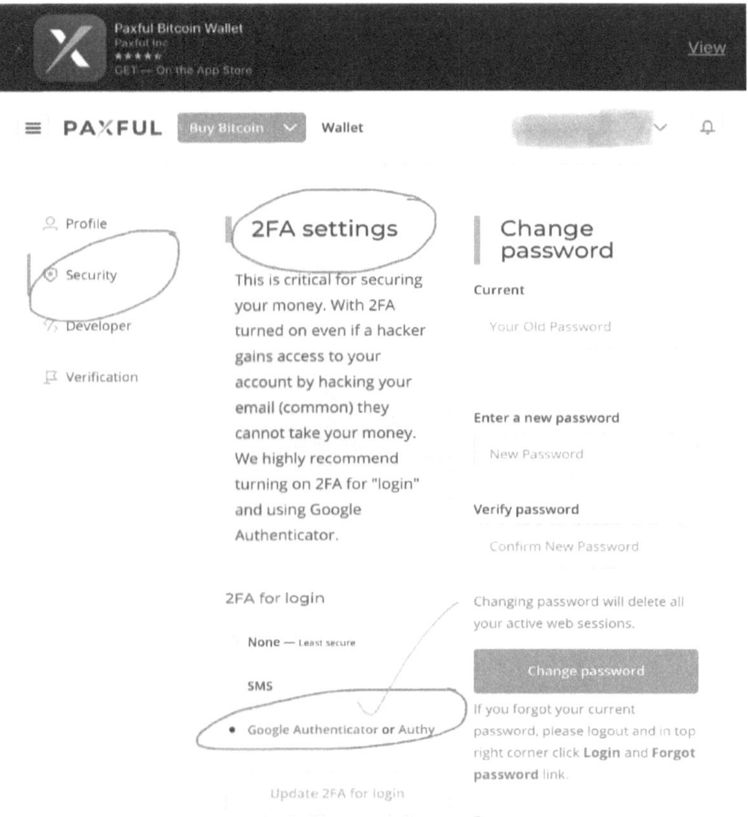

#BE SECURE BE SAFE FROM SCAMMERS

NAMASTE